Cultural Competence

A Guide for Human Service Agencies

Kimberleigh A. Nash

CWLA Press • Washington, DC

CWLA Press is an imprint of the Child Welfare League of America. The Child Welfare League of America (CWLA), the nation's oldest and largest membership-based child welfare organization, is committed to engaging all Americans in promoting the well-being of children and protecting every child from harm.

CHILD WELFARE LEAGUE OF AMERICA, INC.
440 First Street, NW, Third Floor, Washington, DC 20001-2085
E-mail: books@cwla.org

CURRENT PRINTING (last digit)
10 9 8 7 6 5 4 3 2 1

Cover design by Luke Johnson

Printed in the United States of America

ISBN # 0–87868-753-X

Contents

Acknowledgments

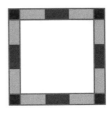

The Child Welfare League of America would like to thank everyone who contributed to the *Advancing Cultural Competence in Child Welfare Initiative*, sponsored by **The Prudential Foundation**. Through this initiative, CWLA has expanded its capacity to assist the child welfare field in providing services and supports to children and families, which are relevant to their cultural values and appropriate to their needs.

CWLA is indebted to The Prudential Foundation for its funding and support of the project, which enabled the research necessary for this guide. We would like to thank them for their continued support of issues that affect the health and well-being of children and families.

Additionally, CWLA would like to thank the advisory committee that worked diligently to produce the consultation pieces for executive leadership and management teams (to which this guide is a companion). This committee enthusiastically provided their experience and expertise that greatly enriched the process of bringing this book to the public. Special thanks go to Sheryl Brissett-Chapman, Nancy E. Cavaluzzi, Frances C. Frazier, Regis G. McDonald, Jean Tucker Mann, Dianne Bostic Robinson, and Layla P. Suleiman.

Dana Burdnell Wilson, director of CWLA's Mid-Atlantic Region and former program director for cultural competence, set the tone and mapped the course for this project from its inception. Her tireless efforts and continued support and greatly appreciated.

Introduction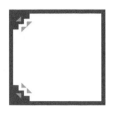

The child welfare field is currently undergoing rapid and dramatic change as it struggles to provide quality services to children and their families. One of the most critical challenges the field faces is the need to understand and respond effectively to changes in the multicultural nature of American society—changes brought about by the mixture of racial, ethnic, social, cultural, and religious traditions of the children and families who make up our diverse society.

These changes, coupled with the demands of a more outcome-driven environment, a more punitive outlook by society on the families served in the child welfare system, an anti-immigration sentiment, and the impact of managed care, challenge today's leaders. Given the range of pressures that impact agencies, child welfare executives face the dilemma of whether to include striving toward cultural competence as an organizational goal.

Currently, children of color are disproportionately represented in the child welfare system, particularly in out-of-home care and in the juvenile justice system. Children of color remain in these systems for longer periods of time and are less likely to be reunited with their families than children of European decent. Children of color in the child welfare system are ethnically diverse and primarily include those of Latino, African American, Asian American, and Native American cultures.

Poverty is the common characteristic among children and families served in child welfare. One in five children in America are poor. The ramifications of poverty—unemployment, inadequate education, inferior or nonexistent health care, substandard housing, and welfare dependence—all increase the likelihood that children in poor families will at some point need the services of the child welfare system.

The increase in the number of people of diverse cultures served by the child welfare system raises the question of which current policies, programs, and services are relevant to the cultural values, traditions, needs, and expectations of the populations served. This is an issue that challenges the child welfare system to extend itself in support of the premise that provision of effective child welfare services is directly related to the knowledge and understanding of, as well as sensitivity and responsiveness to, the culture of the client population. This issue, as well as the formidable task of recruiting and retaining a qualified diverse staff, presents not only challenges, but also opportunities for more effective leadership, management, and service delivery.

Child welfare agencies respond to issues of cultural diversity in many different ways. Many child welfare agency management teams are aggressively shaping an organizational agenda that encompasses a broadened vision; expanded goals and objectives; and modified policies, procedures, and programs to better meet clients' needs. The management teams of these organizations are also attempting to raise their individual comfort levels by gaining an understanding of their own cultural backgrounds and biases, the cultures of others, and multicultural organizational behavior. These management teams are learning how to positively manage the impact of diversity in their organizations—and learning how to celebrate and enjoy the benefits of cultural diversity.

Conversely, many child welfare agencies and management team members are reluctant to develop personal and professional agendas regarding the diverse populations of children and families served by the systems they administer. Many see no need to address the subject of cultural diversity, often because they believe that acknowledging cultural difference could appear to condone discrimination. This "one-size-fits-all" approach denies the existence of the current pluralistic society in the United States, the changing face of child welfare, and the resulting cultural diversity that is an inevitable part of the day-to-day experience.

In response to these challenges, the Child Welfare League of America developed *Advancing Cultural Competence in Child Welfare*, a leadership consultation package that supports child welfare agencies in moving toward cultural competence. The one-day session, designed for executives and board members, is a forum designed to give participants an opportunity to discuss how they themselves may be the dilemmas facing their organizations.

The two-day session, designed for management teams, draws on the knowledge, skills, and experience of the management team members to develop an action plan for including cultural competence in the agency's overall organizational strategic plan. The session helps teams acknowledge the dilemma that cultural competence places on child welfare agencies and seeks to reinforce team members' understanding that movement toward cultural competence is an ongoing process. During this session, management team members explore the various ways cultural competence can be operationalized into the routine duties performed by staff everyday.

CWLA developed this guide, as well as the *Cultural Competence Self-Assessment Instrument,* to assist agencies in their move toward cultural competence.

Why Is Cultural Competence Relevant to an Agency?

CHAPTER 1

When CWLA decided to develop an initiative to assist member agencies as they move toward cultural competence, we realized that a framework was needed that would be flexible and adaptable to any organization, but structured enough to assist agencies with developing and implementing strategies to integrate cultural competence into their overall strategic plan.

As part of this initiative, CWLA set out to develop products that would assist human service organizations who are integrating cultural competence into their child welfare programs, policies, and organizational culture. We began our process as we recommend that you begin yours. First, we had a vision. That vision is our belief that, to effectively and efficiently serve the increasingly diverse populations of this country, child welfare organizations need to become more culturally aware, responsive, and competent.

Our mission was to hold facilitated discussions, communication sessions, and workshops; develop written guides; and conduct consultations that would assist CWLA in moving toward cultural competence.

To reach our mission we set forth the following goals:
- To promote the understanding of cultural competence as an integral part of best practice in child welfare.
- To develop a process that would assist child welfare agencies in moving the organization toward cultural competence.

- To enable child welfare administrators and managers to take the lead in including cultural issues as they plan for positive organizational change.
- To set the stage for ongoing efforts that make effective consultation in cultural competence for child welfare agencies more accessible.

At this point, we must acknowledge the essential tools that enabled us to fulfill our mission and see our vision become reality, and the standards by which decisions in the process were made: our values. Listed below are the values we used in developing the *Advancing Cultural Competence in Child Welfare* initiative:

- Cultural competence is for everyone.
- Cultural competence is integral to best practice.
- Cultural competence is an ongoing process.
- Cultural competence is part of the overall organizational goal of excellence.
- Culturally competent organizations must be customer-driven.
- Cultural competence is a key factor to continued financial survival.
- Culturally competent organizations should foster leadership throughout the organization.

Once we developed the mission, goals, and core values, our next challenge was to build the case for change. We wanted to give child welfare agencies a compelling reason to include cultural competence in their strategic planning process.

There are many reasons why cultural competence is important. Some of those reasons are reflected in the history of child welfare in the United States, and in the current status of the racial/ethnic composition of this country and all over the world.

Over the past 30 years, the United States has experienced a dramatic increase of immigrants from Latin America, the Caribbean, and Asia. All of these people can legitimately call themselves "persons of color." It is estimated that Hispanics/Latinos will be the largest group of people of color in this country by the year 2010.[1] Over the past 10 years, the number of children of European decent has decreased by 10%, the number of African-Americans has increased by 13%, the Latino population has increased by 53%, the Native American population has increased by 37%, and the category "other race" has increased by 45%.[2]

In the 1990 Census, participants used the write-in box to identify almost 300 "races." These races included 600 Indian tribes, 70 Hispanic groups, and 75 combinations of multiracial ancestry.[3] Clearly, Americans are shifting away from the melting pot theory and embracing the various cultures in their backgrounds.

Unlike their predecessors, immigrants entering this country today do not seek assimilation and acculturation into the American "melting pot." They do not want to become "Americans" at the cost of losing their own heritage. Therefore, most have learned how to balance both cultures and function in both worlds.

The diversity of these immigrant populations and the infusion of those cultures into the American mainstream has resulted in many native-born Americans redefining their racial/ethnic descriptors. Native-born Americans have started to identify themselves in terms of their ancestral heritage as opposed to the generic designation; i.e., black or white. As a nation, we have become more concerned about the cultures of our ancestry. We value the richness of the diversity that comprises our personal culture. As we learn to value the different cultures that make up our individual background, we have become more curious about and accepting of different cultures.

Just as diversity has changed the look of our nation, it has dramatically changed the look of the workforce in the United States. It is estimated that by the year 2000, 83% of the workforce will consist of nonwhite people, women, and immigrants.[4] To remain competitive in the marketplace, for-profit and nonprofit organizations alike have had to evaluate how they operate.

The issue of diversity in the work place is becoming more important to for-profit and nonprofit organizations as we enter the next millennium. Changes in the composition of the workforce will require corresponding changes in organizational cultures. To reap the rewards of having a diverse staff, organizations will need to be flexible and look for new ways to include these diverse cultures into organizational operations.

In preparing for the integration of cultural competence into the overall organizational strategic plan, child welfare agencies should go through the following processes:

- Assess the costs and benefits of integrating cultural competence into the vision, mission, values, goals, objectives, policies, procedures, program design, service delivery, and outcomes of the agency.
- Reach consensus as to why an integrated comprehensive approach is the best way to ensure that cultural competence becomes part of the organizational culture.

The systemic, long-term valuing of cultural competence in agencies requires a top-down commitment to an ongoing review of organizational culture. This commitment, both professional and organizational, begins with the tone that is set by the leaders of the organization. The leaders must commit resources—time, people, and money—and make personal and professional commitments to advance cultural competence in the organization. The leaders also take the responsibility for lobbying the board of directors or other governing body to participate in the change process. With this approach, employees may better understand the ongoing nature of the process, and the need for each person in an agency to have a role in moving the organization toward overall competence—a component of which is cultural competence.

Notes

1 Morganthau, T. (1995, February 13). What color is black? *Newsweek*, p. 64.

2 Morganthau, T., p. 64.

3 Morganthau, T., p. 64.

4 Gerber, B. (1990, July 24). Managing diversity. *Training*, p. 24.

How Have Agencies Addressed Difference in the Past?

CHAPTER 2

The field of social work in general and the child welfare system in particular has a history of exclusion and disparity in service delivery for children and families of color. This chapter briefly outlines the struggles African Americans, Native Americans, and Hispanic/Latinos have experienced in the child welfare system.

In the 1960s, the civil rights movement spawned a climate for the development of voluntary agencies to serve African American children and families. Participation by African Americans on the boards of these agencies gave African Americans their first opportunity to control the services delivered to their children and families.[1]

Billingsley and Giovannoni [1972] hypothesized that three factors had caused the increased inclusion of African Americans in the child welfare system since the end of World War II:

> (1) the increased migration by black families to the North, (2) the public system increasingly caring for more poor minority children as the number of poor white children decreased, and (3) the effects of a new national focus on integration.[2]

They believed, however, that the child welfare system continued to treat children of color differently and expressed their belief that "racism was manifested in three ways—by the kinds of services developed, by inequitable treatment based on race within the service delivery system, and by incomplete efforts to change the system."[3]

The authors concluded that, even though there was a concerted effort to eliminate discriminatory practices in child welfare in the 1970s, there still remained an unfair distribution of services, which continued to prevent adequate services from being delivered to African American children and families.

Billingsley and Giovannoni proposed that a pluralistic, multiethnic service delivery system be developed, which would address the needs of all children.[4] While changes were made, access has been increased and services have been improved for children of color, disparity in the allocation of resources continues to be a problem. Stenho's review of Shyne and Shroeder's data collected in 1978 indicated that "a greater proportion of African American children were served in the public sector, and that Caucasian parents received more social service supports than other parents."[5]

The child welfare system has been particularly devastating to Native American children and families. In 1977, 1% of the children in the child welfare system were Native Americans. In 1978, the Children's Defense Fund reported that this number constituted an overrepresentation based on the number of Native American children in the total population.[6] Unger's research found that surveys conducted between 1969 and 1974 "documented that between 25% and 35% of all Native American children were placed in foster or adoptive homes or institutions."[7] Furthermore, Byler's research indicated that 80% of those placements were in Caucasian homes.[8]

Unger noted that Native American children placed in the boarding school system were not allowed to use their native language or observe other cultural customs.[9] A high percentage of transracial placements occurred, because Native American families faced insurmountable obstacles in trying to meet the qualifications for foster and adoptive parents developed by the dominant culture. Olsen's analysis of

Shyne and Shroeder's data indicated that Native American children were the least likely to be recommended for services, while Caucasian and Asian children were most likely to receive services.[10] While controversial and problematic, the passage of the Indian Child Welfare Act in 1978 has at least stemmed the tide of Native American children being placed in homes where they are estranged from their culture.

There has not been as much research done on the history of Latino children in the child welfare system. However, we do know that language and other cultural differences have created barriers for Latino children and families in accessing services. We know that traditionally, Latino children have been transracially placed: lighter skinned children were placed with Caucasian families and darker skinned children were placed with African American families.[11]

This invalidation of their culture has negatively impacted Latino children and may have been the reason for so many being labeled "behaviorally disturbed." People who consider themselves Latino have a wide variety of cultures, which makes placing Latino children more challenging. By placing Latino children in Caucasian and African American homes, the children become even more estranged from their culture and may experience difficulty in acculturating with the foster and/or adoptive family.

Latino children under age 7 were found to be less likely to have service plans than any other group of children.[12] African American and Latino children were least likely to have contact with family members, although there were family members interested in visiting the children. Latino adolescents were more likely to be assessed as having behavioral problems and most likely to be placed in group homes."[13]

Notes

1   Billingsley, A., & Giovannoni, J. M. (1972). *Children of the storm: Black children and American child welfare*. New York: Harcourt Brace Jovanovich. Cited in Hogan, P. T., & Siu, S.-F. (1988, November/December). Minority children and the child welfare system: An historical perspective. *Social Work*, 494.

2   Billingsley & Giovannoni. (1972).

3   Billingsley & Giovannoni. (1972).

4   Billingsley & Giovannoni. (1972).

5   Courtney, M. E., Barth, R. P., Berrick, J. D., Brooks, D., Needell, B., & Park, L. (1996, March/April). Race and child welfare services: Past research and future directions. *Child Welfare*, p. 108.

6   Children's Defense Fund. (1978). *Children without homes: An examination of public responsibility to children in out-of-home care*. Washington, DC: Author. Cited in Hogan, P. T., & Siu, S.-F. (1988, November/December). Minority children and the child welfare system: An historical perspective. *Social Work*, p. 494.

7   Unger, S. (Ed.). (1977). *The destruction of American Indian families*. New York: Association on American Indian Affairs. Cited in Hogan, P. T. & Siu, S.-F. (1988, November/December). Minority children and the child welfare system: An historical perspective. *Social Work*, p. 494.

8   Byler, W. (1977). The destruction of American Indian families. In S. Unger (Ed.), *The destruction of American Indian families* (pp. 1-11). New York Association on American Indian Affairs.

9   Unger. (1977).

10   Olsen, L. J. (1982). Predicting the permanency status of children in foster care. *Social Work Research & Abstracts, 18* (1), 9-20.

11   Montalvo, E. (1994). Against all odds: The challenges faced by Latino families and children in the United States. *The Roundtable*, 8.

12   Montalvo, E. (1994).

13   Montalvo, E. (1994).

What Are the Barriers to and Benefits of a Culturally Competent Organization?

CHAPTER 3

When making the decision to include cultural competence in the strategic plan, many organizations have to weigh the barriers against the benefits.

Barriers in Achieving Cultural Competence

For each organization the barriers and the weight of each may be different. Listed below are some obstacles to cultural competence.

- Cultural competence is hard work.
- There is no "blueprint" for achieving cultural competence.
- Cultural competence requires the commitment of several resources (money, time, and people who are dedicated to the process for a long period of time).
- Cultural competence is like trying to reach infinity, we may come close, but there is always room for work.
- Cultural competence may require major revisions to programs, policies, procedures, and a shift in organizational culture.
- Cultural competence is costly, because every employee will need to go through awareness and skill-based education and ongoing development.
- Organizational size and hierarchical structure can complicate cultural competence.

Benefits to Cultural Competence

Whatever barriers an agency may face in working to achieve cultural competence, the benefits are a constant in the equation:

- Culturally competent agencies are more effective, because they are customer-driven and therefore, understand and respond to the needs of the populations served.
- Culturally competent agencies are more effective, because they reflect the population served in their staffing as well as in the physical environment.
- Culturally competent agencies are more effective, because they value their employees and seek to make them more active in decisions that affect external customers.
- Culturally competent agencies are more effective, because they design programs, policies, and procedures that are sensitive and effective in meeting the needs of the population served in a manner that is most beneficial and acceptable to that population.
- Culturally competent agencies are more effective, because they balance the needs of the organization, employees, and population served to achieve optimal results.
- Culturally competent agencies are more effective, because they attract a larger applicant pool to fill vacancies, and because the organization exhibits an appreciation of diversity and is perceived as a safe place for those seeking a supportive work environment.
- Culturally competent agencies are more effective, because they are more desirable candidates for funders, who are increasingly including cultural competence as a component in grant guidelines.
- Culturally competent agencies are more effective, because they are more likely to receive referrals from other organizations that need to secure assistance and supports for the increasingly diverse populations presenting for services.

What Is the Advantage of a Strategic Plan?

CHAPTER 4

To achieve the maximum benefit, organizations should view cultural competence as an integral part of the strategic planning process. Introducing cultural competence to the organization as a single initiative could give the impression that cultural competence is a special program that will have a definite timeline for completion.

Cultural competence results from a deliberate, systematic, and long-term approach to changing the organization. "Buy-in"—agreement that change is necessary—is not sufficient to initiate or sustain the process in the long-term. Commitment, from the top down, of resources is essential to achieving this goal. Every person at each level of the organization has to be involved and engaged in the process, beginning with the board of directors or other governing body.

A systematic and comprehensive approach is the most effective way of integrating cultural competence into every facet of the organization. A fragmented approach fails to build a strong foundation on which to build the culturally competent agency. The administration of programs, the priorities of the organization, and the basis on which decisions are made impact the cultural competence of an organization. Programs should be administered relative to the needs of the population receiving the services, as opposed to what has worked for other client populations. Organizational priorities and expected outcomes govern how the organization allocates resources. If cultural competence is not a priority, it will most likely not be integrated into the operations of the agency. Moving toward cultural competence requires deliberate planning and should translate into changes in individual and organizational behaviors with demonstrable results.

It is also important for organizations to understand that, like any ongoing process, the cultural competence plan will require periodic review. There may be pieces that have been successfully completed while others need to be initiated, and some will need fine-tuning. Using an assessment tool to perform this periodic review will ensure that the review is comprehensive and will assist in documenting progress and charting a future course. (See Chapter 5 for information on assessment.)

To administer culturally competent services, child welfare agencies need culturally competent staff. The management team, supervisors, social work professionals, administrative support, and other ancillary staff members should be included in awareness and skill-based cultural competence training. From the time a child or family walks in the door of the agency, until their departure, they should encounter people who have the skills to address their needs in a culturally competent manner. The children and families presenting to a child welfare agency need to feel valued and safe.

Agencies can create an atmosphere of familiarity and safety by having staff who are reflective of the population served. In addition, agencies can use furnishings and artwork to reflect the cultural values of the children and families who present for services. Even the magazines ordered for reception areas can contribute to the creation of a safe and hospitable environment.

Agencies that are able to create a safe and comfortable environment are more likely to attract a diverse client population, and are more likely to receive referrals from other human service agencies. In this way, cultural competence affects the fiscal health of the agency.

✳

How Does an Agency Evaluate Itself?

CHAPTER 5

The first step in a strategic planning process is to assess what the agency wants to accomplish by integrating cultural competence into organizational culture and operations. It may be helpful to ask the following questions:

- Is the goal to value diversity or to manage diversity?
- Is the goal to learn more about diversity and be more aware of difference?
- Is the goal to become more efficient and effective in providing services?
- Is the goal to create an environment that fosters open discussion about differences and in which differences are openly addressed in the decision-making process for children and families?

Going through a formal assessment process will help evaluate the entire organization and assess the major issues. Additionally, conducting an assessment will help prioritize the steps in the process. Using a cultural competence assessment tool, such as CWLA's *Cultural Competence Self-Assessment Instrument*, will not only assist you in determining the readiness of the organization for the change process, but will also give you guidance for long-term planning.

An effective cultural competence assessment tool should evaluate the following:

- **The vision, mission, and core values of the organization.** These tools guide the organization and provide the foundation on which decisions that affect the direction of the organization are made. They should be consistent in promoting appropriate and applicable programs, policies, and practice.

- **The composition of the governing body.** The governing body not only leads the organization, but also establishes its priorities. Commitment, not buy-in, is essential in a successful cultural competence process. The governing body that is dedicated to cultural competence should seek to reflect the diversity of the organization and population served in its membership. This will send a strong message that cultural competence is important to the organization. A culturally competent governing body will also be more effective in developing a strategic plan for the organization, a plan that values differences and is effective in meeting the needs of all stakeholders. To the extent possible, governing bodies should recruit members from the community served, as well as representatives from other stakeholder groups.

- **The selection process for selecting governing body members.** The criteria that are used to select governing body members can impact the diversity of the group. Who is solicited for membership and what is done to connect new members to the group and retain established members can determine whether diversity is achieved.

- **Governing body orientation and ongoing education processes.** In this constantly changing environment, ongoing education is important to keep the governing body abreast of what is occurring in the marketplace and how the organization can align itself to meet the changing needs of the population served.

- **Criteria on which leaders are selected to run the organization.** Because of the complexity of the role of executive, most organizations believe that there is a small pool of qualified candidates. There are many qualified people with good ideas and the ability to make them happen. To reach this pool of talent, however, organizations need to be creative in their search process. Sometimes organizations establish requirements for leadership positions that screen out interested and capable candidates. Length of time in a leadership position does not necessarily equal success in the position.

Leadership

The following are useful criteria in selecting a leader who values cultural competence:

- the ability to create a climate for excellence
- the ability to provide a safe environment for the discussion of differences and the constructive exchange of ideas and information
- the ability to inspire and motivate people to achieve and excel
- the ability to take risks with comfort
- a belief that customer service and satisfaction, both internal and external, are the most important factors in a healthy organization
- a belief that change is inevitable and should be embraced and encouraged

Note that these are also desirable qualities for any person being hired in a managerial capacity. The difference is that a person who values cultural competence will use these strengths to enhance the organization by bringing new voices to the organization. This person will be the catalyst for diversifying the staff, creating innovative programs, policy, and practice, improving communication throughout the organization, and encouraging more interaction with the population served in ways that improve outcomes.

Leaders must be personally dedicated to the constant growth and development of skills and knowledge. The need to be results-driven and be able to get people to deliver the desired results is essential. The personality and values of a person are key factors in determining whether he or she can achieve the desired results of the organization. Someone who fits well with the vision, mission, and core values of the organization will be in a better position to meet the expectations of the organization.

Programs, Policy, and Practice

To be successful at delivering culturally competent services and supports, child welfare agencies must make sure internal policies and procedures are culturally competent. It is not enough to send line staff and supervisors to cultural competence educational sessions. The organization needs to work toward a total agency goal of cultural competence. This includes making appropriate educational sessions available to all internal stakeholders, improving relationships with the community, developing effective internal policies, and designing programs and case management systems that are appropriate and applicable to the population served.

Policies, Procedures, and Personnel Manuals

Policies and procedures should be flexible. Part of valuing diversity is understanding that flexibility is a key factor in cultural competence. Every situation does not lend itself to a consistent and neat answer. To achieve diversity, organizations and people need to be creative and innovative in creating policies and procedures. Personnel manuals are important to cultivating and maintaining cultural competence in the workplace. Cultural competence should be a consideration from the time of posting a vacant position through the employee's exit interview. Cultural competence should be built into how job descriptions and job announcements are written and include, but not be limited to, performance evaluations, disciplinary actions, work hours, and how leave can be used.

Program Development Guidelines

Flexibility should be a key ingredient in the development of programs. Programs administered in such a way that they are responsive to the needs of the population(s) served will have better outcomes for the customer and the staff who deliver services. Information gathered in customer satisfaction surveys or focus groups can be helpful in this process. Including all levels of staff and consumer representation on program design committees will also help ensure that the needs and expectations of both internal and external customers are met.

Case Management

Services are to be delivered with respect, ultimately seeking to build upon family strengths. Service plans should be done in partnership with the families' served, acknowledging that they are more expert in knowing what they need. Agencies should establish clear responsibilities with regard to both family activities and agency activities. Attention to accessibility of appropriate services should be consistent.

Recruitment and Retention Strategies

Organizations should be innovative in how they recruit for vacancies. To enhance diversity, organizations should consider a variety of avenues to recruit staff. Using publications targeted to specific groups and relationships with community organizations can enhance the ability to hire staff that are culturally diverse and competent. To retain employees, organizations have to create an environment where difference is valued and where the discussion of difference is safe and constructive.

Additionally, there are incentives that organizations can offer to attract and maintain staff. For example, mentoring and career pathing are two options. Mentoring programs can be formatted in many ways and are quite helpful in assisting new employees to adjust to the organization. Mentoring is another vehicle through which the organization can communicate the organizational vision, mission, goals, and culture.

Career pathing is a concept many organizations are using to retain employees. Career pathing requires a considerable amount of planning on the part of organization, but can have excellent results. To be effective, each position in the organization should have a career path—an established route that employees could follow to move vertically in the organization. This pathing could be shared with new employees as a benefit of joining the organization.

Relationship with the Community and Public Image

The perception of the organization in the community, as well as the location of the agency, is crucial to determining who applies for positions and who requests services. Organizations that have staff involved in the community they serve (i.e., that participate on community advisory boards, cultivate relationships with the faith community or civic groups, and serve on agency boards and committees) have a more positive image and are more attractive to customers and staff.

Appropriateness and Effectiveness of Publications

Publications should reflect the populations served in content and design. Publications in different languages, with photographs, graphics, or other artwork, should reflect the diversity of the population served. Additionally, publications should be designed to have the most positive impact on those who will access and read them.

Outcome Evaluations

As child welfare agencies become more outcome-based, they need to establish evaluation guidelines. It is important for child welfare agencies and professionals to know how the populations they serve are impacted by the programs administered. Desired outcomes should be identified for each program area. These outcomes should be measurable and relate to how children and families are affected. The delivery of appropriate services that produce desired outcomes is cost effective. Delivering services that do not meet the needs of the population ultimately means that additional services will be required to produce the desired results.

Advocacy

Often, the child welfare agency has an interest in both providing services to children and families, and in advocating on their behalf. This may be operationalized through service workers who advocate for customers in seeking needed services from other agencies (i.e., health care, special education, parenting support), as well as through service organizations that advocate on behalf of a population of families in the public policy area. Child welfare executives and managers may find that a specific cultural issue is the driving force behind the decision to initiate an advocacy effort. Potentially, many will benefit from this effort spurred by a few, when the result is more respectful, effective, and relevant services for children and families.

Internal and External Customer Feedback

Organizations that are effective in any change process have solicited, received, processed, and made revisions based on the feedback of internal and external customers. Organizations who have sustained long-term growth credit keeping an open ear to their customers as the reason they continue to be successful in the market place. External customers are the ultimate judge of effectiveness; however, internal customers have valuable insight into how to improve services because they have a dual vantage point.

Frontline staff who deliver services are aware of the organizational goals, objectives, and intentions as well as the perception, impression, priorities, and effectiveness of the services provided by the agency. This wealth of information can assist agencies in prioritizing and focusing the change process. It also has the residual benefit of making both the internal and external customer feel valued and important to the organization and they are included in this ongoing process.

What the Organization Has Done to Value the Diversity of the Workforce and the Population Served

Many organizations have recognized the need for change and are actively working on cultural competence initiatives. In this situation, the foundation is under construction and decisions have been made regarding the desired outcomes of the change process. What is important is that these organizations understand that this is a constantly evolving process that has no finite point of destination. As the organization grows and changes, so will the needs of the population(s) served. Thus the organization continues to evolve and continuously deliver appropriate, effective, and responsive services.

Volunteer Recruitment, Selection, and Orientation

Volunteers have an important and unique role in child welfare organizations. While their desire to provide assistance is an asset to the agency, the volunteers' lack of formal connection to the agency may present some challenges. It is important that volunteers understand and are a suitable fit with the mission, values, goals, objectives, and organizational culture of the agency. Volunteers should be included in the plan to integrate cultural competence in the overall agency strategic plan.

Volunteers should possess the same interpersonal skills required of staff members, especially if they will have contact with the children and families served by the agency. Evaluative criteria should be established to ensure that they are a good fit with the organization and the tasks they will be asked to perform. Additionally, volunteers should be included in in-service training and in ongoing developmental training, evaluation, and feedback processes.

Recruitment, Selection, Orientation, and Training of Foster and Adoptive Parents

Foster and adoptive parents hold key roles in the child welfare system. Children unable to remain in their own home must have a safe, stable, nurturing home with another family. As caregivers, foster and adoptive parents will play a critical role in the development of the child; therefore, the selection, orientation, and training of these caregivers will directly affect the health, welfare, and happiness of the child. While there continues to be debate around the issue of transracial placements and adoptions, what is clear is that children thrive in stable, caring, loving homes.

CWLA emphasizes the early achievement of an appropriate permanency goal for each child. Furthermore, CWLA encourages agencies to make every effort to place children in homes that are consistent with the child's ethnicity and culture, past identifications, and living experiences. In cases where all reasonable efforts have been made over a period of time to find parents of the same ethnicity and culture as the child, CWLA supports the identification of another suitable family to provide a home for the child. When a child is placed transracially, however, agencies should assess the ability of the foster/adoptive parents to access cultural resources to support the child and family after the placement.

The ability of an agency to recruit and retain a diverse pool of foster and adoptive parents who can create and maintain an environment that is supportive to the total development of a child is invaluable. Recruiting guidelines for foster and adoptive parents should reflect the understanding that there are several factors which make a good parent, a good home, and a good family. There is no "model family" that creates the best environment for the rearing of children.

Single parents, gay/lesbian parents, parents who work outside the home, and those who do not earn a lot of money, should not be excluded from consideration.

All foster and adoptive parents should go through training to learn how to deal with the many feelings and issues that arise by opening their home to a foster/adoptive child. They should be required to demonstrate the ability to be flexible and resourceful in assisting the child to connect with his/her culture. Even where there is no racial or ethnic difference between adoptive/foster parent and child, other cultural issues may exist that require the foster/adoptive parent to be resourceful in creating a healthy, loving, caring, and stable environment for the child.

Organizational Culture

Every organization has an unwritten set of rules, or organizational culture. How the organization functions and what the organization values is part of the culture of the organization. Agencies striving for cultural competence strive to attain a level of openness that supports a discussion of difference. The organizational culture has to value difference, learning, growth, and change. Successful agencies take the "that's the way we have always done it" mentality and replace it with a "if it makes us more efficient, effective, and responsive, let's work on it" mentality.

Needs of the Population

When assessing the needs of the populations served by the organization, several factors must be taken into consideration. Our individual culture is shaped by a variety of factors. Contrary to popular belief, an individual's racial/ethnic group may not be the aspect of his/her culture to which s/he most strongly identifies. Therefore, when organizations begin designing policies, procedures, personnel manuals, programs, service delivery plans, publications, etc., the following should be considered:

- religion
- language
- education
- gender roles
- intergenerational dynamics
- beliefs regarding help from outside the family unit
- parenting norms
- beliefs regarding health care
- sexual orientation
- mental health issues
- vision or hearing impairment
- physical challenges
- racism
- ethnicity
- geographic location of the organization
- the time period when individuals were born
- geographic location of rearing and/or current place of domicile
- family values
- self-determination
- placement in sibling group
- race

The assessment process can be extremely complex, but it is the foundation for learning and understanding who works in and who is served by the organization. The time it takes to collect these data to get an accurate picture of the agency will be well worth the effort as the agency goes through the process of striving for cultural competence.

How Does an Agency Develop an Action Plan?

CHAPTER 6

Once the organization has completed the assessment, the next step is to develop an action plan. The decisions made in developing the action plan and the priority assigned to each task will grow out of the information learned in the assessment process.

The action plan should consist of "doable" tasks and realistic timelines. Most importantly, the action plan should be inclusive, assigning tasks to staff at all levels of the organization. Inclusion, through communication and involvement, will increase employees' ownership of the process and build loyalty to the organization while promoting unity both horizontally and vertically. There should be representation from all stakeholder groups in the process. You should not only solicit input from stakeholders, but also request their active participation in transforming the organization.

Include staff from all levels of the organization in all phases of the process. Distribute leadership, accountability, and responsibility among the entire staff. Allowing those not normally in leadership roles to be responsible for the development, design, and implementation of parts of the process will encourage staff to be concerned about the agency as a whole, as opposed to just the area in which they work.

Many times, leaders in the organization are reluctant to give line staff opportunities to be decisionmakers. Don't be afraid of empowering these employees to use their creativity and insight to design

more culturally competent policies, programs, and practice direc-
tives. The worst they can do is make some poor choices. Remember—managers, directors, and other leaders have also made poor
choices. There is strength in including into the process the views,
thoughts, concerns, and insights of those least approached for this
kind of information. Don't overlook your resources and assets and
don't miss an opportunity to foster leadership throughout the organization!

The action plan should address the dilemmas facing the organization that have cultural implications. (These dilemmas should have
surfaced during the assessment process.) You can also glean additional information from customer satisfaction surveys and focus
groups developed for each stakeholder group.

The most important thing is to remember that change is gradual
and takes time. It is important for all stakeholders to be a part of the
process from planning to implementation, and it is crucial that tasks
be doable and timelines realistic. If you get sidetracked, a good plan
will help bring the process back in line. Change can sometimes be
painful and difficult in organizations. Keep in mind, however, that
without change there cannot be growth.

How Does Change Happen?

CHAPTER 7

Children are our future, and as we go into a new millennium, child welfare professionals should find ways to embrace the change. Our job is to make sure that the future of children is better in the twenty-first century than it is now. Our future includes an increasingly diverse population of people in this country. Taking steps to meet the new challenges now will prepare your organization to continue to champion the cause for children.

For the agency whose goal is to value diversity, two change processes must occur simultaneously: an organizational change process and a behavioral change process. This chapter outlines the steps in those two processes.

Organizational Change

The change process that moves organizations toward cultural competence is much the same as any change management strategy. While the steps may be the same, the outcome should be driven by a sincere desire to build an organization that is not only capable of delivering appropriate and applicable services to the population(s) served, but also has internal policies and practices that create a safe and supportive environment for internal stakeholders. Cultural competence should permeate the agency in every aspect of how the organization functions.

Culturally competent programs and policies cannot be written in a vacuum. They should be the result of a deeper understanding and an effort to create a better organization for staff, consumers, and other stakeholders.

- Evaluate current conditions and decide that change is needed.
- Decide exactly what needs to be changed and develop a plan to achieve those changes.
- Develop a case for change or compelling reason that the change needs to occur to generate discussion within the organization. Such discussion will facilitate the buy-in and commitment of everyone in the organization.
- Develop result-oriented strategies for achieving change.
- Institute mechanisms to keep change process moving and on target, as well as to collect and respond to feedback.
- Involve key stakeholders in the change process and give them specific tasks to ensure commitment and success.
- Make sure that resources (money, time, people, mission, values, goals, policies, and procedures) are in place to assist the organization in facilitating the change process and attaining the desired results.
- Integrate the changes into the operations of the organization.
- Evaluate the new process at regular intervals for modification and reinforcement.
- Continuously look for ways to improve the organizational culture and operations.

Behavioral Change

Organizations are built by and for people. The integration of cultural competence into any agency requires a change in behavior, both organizational and individual. The normal process of this change includes the following steps:

- A change in thinking, a new awareness and understanding, acceptance of different attitudes, beliefs, values, and perceptions;

- A change in actions accompanied by a clear and realistic plan for changing practice; and
- A change in habit as the commitment to the new way of thinking and acting increases.

Long-lasting, effective change cannot occur without both individual and organizational changes in behavior. Relationships between stakeholders will transform, individually and collectively, to achieve sustained movement toward cultural competence.

- Introduce a catalyst or stimulus for change.
- Process the new information and evaluate how that new information challenges established thoughts, beliefs, values, and behaviors.
- Decide what kind of action should be taken to modify and/or correct behavior to be in line with the new environment
- Practice the new actions and thinking patterns until they become a habit that is then integrated into behaviors.

Other Factors in the Change Process

You should consider several factors that will have an impact on how decisions are made, which services are provided, and how the best outcomes can be attained.

Race and ethnicity are the two most obvious concerns in cultural competence, because they are the easiest to recognize. Many of the issues that surround cultural competence clearly result from differences in race and ethnicity. Majority and minority orientation conflicts are the root of many problems experienced between people. There are no easy answers to this problem, and it continues to be an emotional and provocative issue. We ask that organizations and individuals recognize that there are many other factors also at play and investigate the possibility that those factors also complicate the ability to provide services.

Intergenerational and Gender Roles

A hierarchical family structure governs the interaction between family members, as well as those outside the family. It is important for child welfare organizations and professionals to understand that these dynamics exist and learn to work within that structure. Child welfare professionals should ascertain who is the head or leader of the family unit and work with them to give assistance to the child and remainder of the family.

Where language barriers exist, it is usually not a good idea to have a younger family member serve as an interpreter, because this places the child in a adult role and involves them in an adult conversation. This makes the parent feel powerless and resentful of the process. For these cases, a bilingual staff member or a translator will make interaction with the family go more smoothly.

Gender role definition, coupled with intergenerational dynamics, creates an environment in which children learn values, interpersonal interaction skills, and appropriate behavior.

Having positive and effective interactions with children and families requires that child welfare organizations and professionals respect family structure and design policies, procedures, programs, and service delivery and case management plans that are easily adaptable to a wide range of family structures and dynamics. The person who needs to obtain services may not be the person first contacted or talked to in determining which services should be provided. Ignoring those who are not readily apparent as important in the family structure may create distrust and might cause children and families to be noncompliant with the management plan.

Education

In this country, a person's educational level usually determines his or her ability to survive economically. However, formal education does not ensure the ability to provide appropriate parenting, and, conversely, the lack of education does not equate to poor parenting skills. (Additionally, the affluence of a parent has no direct correlation as to the quality of parenting that will be provided.) Therefore, child welfare organizations and professionals should look for other criteria that can assist them in making decisions around the ability to provide adequate parenting.

Parenting

Parenting norms vary from culture to culture without the uniformity found in intergenerational and gender roles. Parenting roles vary widely between cultures—what may be acceptable in one is perceived as inappropriate or harmful in another. When confronted with different methods of parenting, child welfare professionals should first seek to understand the purpose of the parent's behavior in response to the child's. Once a child welfare professional understands the purpose for the parent's behavior, a more informed case management plan can be drafted and more appropriate services given to the child and family.

Communication

Communication is another barrier to providing services to children and families. Whether it is a different language or a visual or hearing impairment, organizations need to make provisions for communicating with children and families through the medium that is most comfortable for them. This can be accomplished by providing training and encouraging staff to be bilingual, and by hiring bilingual staff and those skilled in sign language. If staff cannot fulfill these needs, then the agencies should contract these services from outside vendors.

Additionally, publications about the agency and the services offered should be developed in the language(s) of the population(s) served, in braille, and on audiotape where appropriate.

Communication styles and patterns differ by cultural group. What may be acceptable communication to one group may be offensive to another. Child welfare professionals should be aware that these differences exist and identify the best way to communicate with the populations served by the agency.

Homelessness

Homelessness is a growing problem in this country, with families being the fastest growing segment of the homeless population. Providing a safe, stable, loving, and nurturing environment is difficult enough. Homelessness creates a set of complex challenges that require agencies and child welfare professionals to be more innovative and flexible in their approach to achieving positive outcomes.

Sexual Orientation

Sexual orientation has been at the root of many custody battles recently. Research indicates, however, that gay and lesbian natural, adoptive, and foster parents are just as capable of providing a caring, nurturing, supportive, and stable home as heterosexual parents. Children reared by gay and lesbian parents are no more likely to become gay and lesbian than those reared in heterosexual homes. For these reasons, and the fact that the number of parents volunteering as foster and adoptive parents is shrinking, agencies need to consider gays and lesbians as a viable and appropriate choice for providing temporary and permanent homes for children.

Research has shown that gay and lesbian youth are more likely to be depressed and to attempt or commit suicide. They sustain more abuse from peers and are often ostracized by their families. Child welfare professionals should provide support and link these youth into other sources of support in the community.

Religion

Religious beliefs play a major role in some cultures in determining how children are reared, how family members interact with one another as well as how they interact with those outside the family unit. It is important for child welfare professionals to take this into account when designing programs, policies, and procedures.

Health Care Practices

Beliefs around health care can also create barriers in providing services to families. These beliefs often stem from religious beliefs, lack of education, fear of strangers and large systems, or language barriers. Organizations and child welfare professionals should first identify the reason the family is not seeking health care and then work with the family and health care providers to achieve the best outcome, while respecting the cultural and religious beliefs of the family.

Juvenile Delinquency

Research on the juvenile justice system has documented that children of color who commit delinquent acts are more likely to be adjudicated in the juvenile justice system, while children of European descent usually are given mental health services. Because of the negative impact this trend has on children of color, child welfare professionals need to work in conjunction with the juvenile justice system to evaluate the criteria on which decisions are made. Failure to find more appropriate solutions to addressing juvenile crime will result in a disproportionate number of children of color being reared in correctional facilities.

Female youth are another group increasing in numbers in the juvenile justice system. The National Center for Juvenile Justice reported in 1996 that between 1989 and 1993, the number of arrests reported for girls increased by 23%. The arrest rate for girls committing violent crimes during that same period increased by 125%. During that same period of time, the rate for boys increased by 67%. Additionally, the report stated that 50% to 70% of the girls arrested had been sexually and/or physically abused.[1] Before this trend gets

worse, child welfare professionals need to find ways of more ad-
equately addressing the factors that cause these young women to
become involved in crime.

Notes

1 Mehren, E. (1996, May 17). As bad as they wanna be. *Los Angeles Times*,
   E.

How Does an Agency Involve the Community?

CHAPTER 8

Image is everything; perception is reality! How an agency is seen by those who are served is critical to the ability of the agency to positively impact the outcomes for children and families.

If the population served perceives that their concerns are not heard when they present for services, they either won't come or will not comply with the case management plan. Organizations have to value and respect the community to be valued and respected themselves. Being involved in the community also allows the community to be involved in the organization. Recognizing the community as important stakeholders in the change process and inviting community members to participate in the development stage is an excellent step toward building a relationship with the community. This also gives the agency valuable information about what the community needs and expects from the agency. Listed below are some strategies that can enhance community relationships:

- Invite community members to come to the agency to learn about the staff, services, and operations.
- Survey the population served and the community at large to get feedback about services provided and to ascertain desires and expectations.
- Ask community leaders to sit on the board of directors and/or other agency task forces and committees.

- Conduct focus groups and other activities designed to get input from the community about what the agency is doing well and where improvement is needed.
- Participate in community functions and activities and, when possible, work collaboratively or in partnership with community groups.
- Express a desire to be involved as members of community advisory boards and civic groups.
- Invite community members to periodically speak to the board of directors about services, needs, and expectations.
- Establish formal liaisons between the organization and the community.
- Focus recruitment efforts to increase numbers of staff from the community.

How Does an Agency Practice Cultural Competence Among Its Staff?

CHAPTER 9

Providing exceptional services to external customers is the ultimate goal for any child welfare agency. To meet that goal, the organization has to begin with itself, and focus on how to develop good internal customer service.

What is internal customer service? Organizations have internal customers, either as individuals or as groups/divisions/departments. Each individual/division/department has customers and is also a customer to another individual/division/department. The interdependency of the organization creates the customer relationships. Each person/division/department needs information, services, or products from another to perform effectively and efficiently and to achieve the desired outcomes.

Some examples of internal customer relationships are the person who orders the supplies, and the individual who requests supplies; the worker who receives a case, and the worker who transfers the case. Another example is the executive who sees the need for a change in organizational operations, organizes a multidisciplinary group to decide what the change affects, how the change will be accomplished, what the expected outcomes are, and what role each person in the organization will play. Good internal customer service is crucial to providing good external customer service.

Some of the same factors that are important in understanding and valuing diversity in the development of programs, policies, and procedures are equally important in the recruitment and retention of staff. As the workforce becomes more culturally diverse, there will be a new set of factors that affect what motivates employees and how the organization functions.

Race and ethnicity, intergenerational and gender roles, parenting norms, communications, sexual orientation, level of education, and religion will impact the work environment in the same ways they affect the decisions made regarding the development of programs, policies, and procedures for the population served.

Value and respect your staff; celebrate and incorporate their cultural differences into how the organization functions. Give considerations to these differences when personnel policies and procedures are being drafted, when job descriptions are written, when salaries are increased, when the holiday schedule is determined, etc.

To be successful in the cultural competence change process means that everyone in an organization is willing to learn about difference and to allow for the adjustments that are necessary as the agency moves toward cultural competence.

Conclusion

CHAPTER 10

Cultural competence is a process. It requires a commitment of resources—money, people, and time—to be successful. Organizations striving for cultural competence need to plan, be persistent, and remain flexible throughout the process. Change takes time. As organizations move through the process toward cultural competence, no doubt they will encounter other external forces that challenge their ability to deliver appropriate and relevant services.

Making cultural competence an organizational priority, however, is a part of overall organizational competence. The integration of cultural competence in the strategic planning process is integral to best practice and has implications for fiscal survival. Cultural competence is an inclusive concept and is for everyone. We all need to work individually and collectively to understand, respect, and celebrate the richness that difference brings to our lives and the workplace.

As we move into a new millennium, child welfare agencies must prepare to meet the increasing demands, by consumers, for appropriate and applicable services and supports. As the composition of our general population becomes more diverse, so will the needs of the children and families served by the child welfare system. If child welfare agencies truly want to help each child and family reach their full potential, they must be prepared to embrace culture and difference. To reach this goal, however, child welfare agencies must under-

41

stand that diversity begins within an organization. Therefore, the agencies that want to attract and retain the best talent in the field must demonstrate the ability to provide a safe and comfortable environment, where difference is valued.

Resources

Adoption/Foster Care

Gilles, T., & Kroll, J. (1991, April). *Barriers to same race placement.* St. Paul, MN: The North American Council on Adoptable Children.

Kallgren, C. A., & Caudill, P. J. (1993). Current transracial adoption practices: Racial dissonance or racial awareness? *Psychological Reports, 72,* 551-558.

Sullivan, A. (1994). Update on transracial adoption. *Children's Voice, 3,* 4-6.

Child Protective Services

Ahn, H. N., & Gilbert, N. (1992, September). Cultural diversity and sexual abuse prevention. *Social Service Review, 66,* 410-427.

Dore, M. M., Doris, J. M., & Wright, P. (1995, May). Identifying substance abuse in maltreating families: A child welfare challenge. *Child Abuse and Neglect, 19,* 531-543.

Finkelhor, D. (1993, January/February). Epidemiological factors in the clinical identification of child sexual abuse. *Child Abuse and Neglect, 17,* 67-70.

Leung, P., Cheung, K-F. M., & Stevenson, K. M. (1994, November/December). A strengths approach to ethnically sensitive practice for child protective service workers. *Child Welfare, 73,* 707-721.

Stevenson, K., Cheung, K-F. M., & Leung, P. (1992, July/August). A new approach to training child protective service workers for ethnically sensitive practice. *Child Welfare, 71,* 291-303.

Disabilities

Beck, R. L. (1989, March). Hearing-impaired social workers: Something lost, something gained. *Social Work, 34*, 151-153.

Dickert, J. (1988, May/June). Examination of bias in mental health evaluation of deaf patients. *Social Work, 33*, 273-274.

Luey, H. S., Glass, L., & Elliott, H. (1995, March). Hard-of-hearing or deaf: Issues of ears, language, culture, and identity. *Social Work, 40*, 177-181.

Sarti, D. M. (1993, March). Reaching the deaf child: A model for diversified intervention. *Smith College Studies in Social Work, 63*, 187-197.

HIV/AIDS

Stevenson, H. C., Jr. (1994, September). The psychology of sexual racism and AIDS: An ongoing saga of distrust and the sexual other. *Journal of Black Studies, 25*, 62-80.

Youth & HIV/AIDS: An American agenda. A report to the President. (1996, March). Prepared by the Office of National AIDS Policy, Sponsored by the National AIDS Fund through grants from the Until There's A Cure Foundation and James C. Hormel Fund.

Juvenile Justice

Bishop, D. M., & Fazier, C. E. (1988, August). Influence of race in juvenile justice processing. *Journal of Research in Crime and Delinquency, 25*, 242-263.

Fagan, J., Slaughter, E., & Hartstone, E. (1987, April). Blind justice? The impact of race on the juvenile justice process. *Crime and Delinquency, 33*, 224-258.

Mehren, E. (1996, May 17). As bad as they wanna be. *Los Angeles Times/ Orange County Edition*, Section E.

Ohlin, L. E. (1983, July). The future of juvenile justice policy and research. *Crime and Delinquency*, 463-472.

Westendorp, F., Brink, K. L., Roberson, M. K., & Ortiz, I. E. (1986, Spring). Variables which differentiate placement of adolescents into juvenile justice or mental health systems, *Adolescence, 21*, 23-35.

Managed Care

Doty, D. (1995). Can foster care services be managed? *Open Minds, 8*, 4-5.

Drissel, A. (1997, March). Managed care & child welfare: Trends, issues, and challenges in 1997. *The Children's Vanguard, 1*, 1-2.

McCullough C., & Langley, K. (1996, August). States eye managed care for child welfare reform. *Open Minds, 10*, 4-5.

Moravec, M. (1996, Autumn). Linking reengineering to revitalization. *Managed Care Quarterly, 4*, 106-112.

Roizner, M. (1996). *A practical guide for the assessment of cultural competence in children's mental health organizations: The technical assistance center for the evaluation of children's mental health systems.* Boston, MA: Judge Baker Children's Center.

Organizational Development

Anthony, D., Carnevale, P., & Stone, S. C. (1994, October). Diversity: Beyond the golden rule. *Training & Development*, 22-39.

Fram, E. F., & Pearse, R. F. (1992). *The high-performance nonprofit: A management guide for boards and executives.* Milwaukee, WI: Family Service America, Inc.

Geber, B. (1990, July). Managing diversity. *Training*, 23-30.

Goldstein, J., & Leopold, M. (1990, November). Corporate culture versus ethnic culture. *Personnel Journal*, 83-92.

Jamieson. D., & O'Mara, J. (1991). *Managing Workforce 2000: Gaining the diversity advantage.* San Francisco, CA: Jossey-Bass, Inc.

Rutledge, J. M. (1994). *Building board diversity.* Washington, DC: National Center for Nonprofit Boards.

Thomas, D. A., & Ely, R. J. (1996, September/October). Making differences matter: A new paradigm for managing diversity. *Harvard Business Review, 74*, 79-90.

Race & Racism

Courtney, M. E., Barth, R. P., Berrick, J. D., Brooks, D., Needell, B., & Park, L. (1996, March/April). Race and child welfare services: Past research and future directions. *Child Welfare, 75*, 99-137.

Kinder, D. R., & Mendelberg, T. (1995, May). Cracks in American apartheid: The political impact of prejudice among desegregated whites. *The Journal of Politics, 57*, 402-24.

Katlin, F. (1982, March). The impact of ethnicity. *Social Casework, 63*, 168-171.

Abernethy, A. D. (1995, April). Managing racial anger: A critical skill in cultural competence. *Journal of Multicultural Counseling and Development, 23*, 96-101.

McIntosh, P. (1989, July/August). White privilege: Unpacking the invisible knapsack. *Peace and Freedom*, 10-11.

Sexual Orientation

Morrow, D. F. (1993, November). Social work with gay and lesbian adolescents. *Social Work, 38*, 655-660.

O'Connell, A. (1993, June). Voices from the heart: The developmental impact of a mother's lesbianism on her adolescent children. *Smith College in Social Work, 63*, 281-299.

Rotheram-Borus, M. J., Rasario, M., Reid, H., & Koopman, C. (1995, April). Predicting patterns of sexual acts among homosexual and bisexual youth. *American Journal of Psychiatry, 152*, 588-594.

Tasker, F., & Golombok, S. (1995, April). Adults raised as children in lesbian families. *American Journal of Orthopsychiatry, 65*, 203-215.

Social Work

Berger, R. (1989, July). Promoting minority access to the profession. *Social Work*, 346-349.

Brissett-Chapman, S. (1994). Ethical dilemmas: A moral framework for leadership and decision making. *The Child and Youth Care Administrator, 6*, 23-25.

Cross, T. L., Bazron, B. J., Dennis, K. W., & Issacs, M. R. (1989, March). Towards a culturally competent system of care, Volume I. Washington, DC: CASSP Technical Assistance Center at Georgetown University Child Development Center.

Mann, J. T. (1994). Diversity: Professional and personal challenges for executive leadership. *The Child and Youth Care Administrator, 6*, 20-22.

Manoleas, P. (1994). Social work: An outcome approach to assessing the cultural competence of MSW students. *Journal of Multicultural Social Work, 3*, 43-57.

Pancost, R. (1994). Ten reasons for the increase in executive stress. *The Child and Youth Care Administrator, 6*, 11-15.

Preli, R., & Bernard, J. M. (1993, January). Making multiculturalism relevant for majority culture graduate students. *Journal of Marital and Family Therapy, 19*, 5-16.

Sanders, D. S. (1980). Multiculturalism: Implications for social work. *International Social Work, 23*, 9-16.

For More Information

For more information about cultural competence, please contact

Kimberleigh A. Nash
Director of Special Projects and
Program Coordinator, Cultural Competence
Child Welfare League of America
440 First Street, NW, Third Floor
Washington, DC 20001-2085
202/942-0319
E-mail: knash@cwla.org

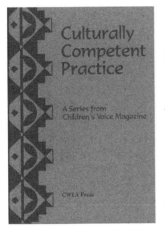

Culturally Competent Practice: A Series from Children's Voice Magazine

A reprint of the four-part series, "Culturally Competent Practice," this collection investigates the unique cultural values that child and family practitioners should keep in mind when working with families of different ethnic backgrounds. Sections include:

- Asian family values from the perspective of Buddhism, Confucianism, and Taoism
- The strengths—and myths—of African American families
- A challenge for agencies to develop programs that better fit the Latino cultural mosaic
- Family treatment and healing within the relational world view of Native American culture

Cultural Competence

Self-Assessment

Instrument

This popular field-tested management tool will help child service organizations identify, improve, and enhance cultural competence in staff relations and client service delivery. With a practical, easy-to-use approach, it addresses the major issues of delivering culturally competent service. Users will be able to determine whether or not existing agency policies, practices, and programs achieve and promote cultural competence in the areas of governance, program development, administration, management, and service delivery.

How to order CWLA resources on cultural competence

To order

Culturally Competent Practice:
A Series from Children's Voice Magazine

1998/0-87868-704-1/#7041 $8.95

Write:	CWLA	Call:	800/407-6273
	P.O. Box 2019		301/617-7825
	Annapolis Junction, MD 20701		
e-mail:	cwla@pmds.com	Fax:	301/206-9789

Please specify stock #7041. Bulk discount policy (not for resale): 10-49 copies 10%, 50-99 copies 20%, 100 or more copies 40%. Canadian and foreign orders must be prepaid in U.S. funds. MasterCard/Visa accepted.

To order

Cultural Competence Self-Assessment Instrument

1993/0-87868-506-5/#5065 $25.95

Write:	CWLA	Call:	800/407-6273
	P.O. Box 2019		301/617-7825
	Annapolis Junction, MD 20701		
e-mail:	cwla@pmds.com	Fax:	301/206-9789

Please specify stock #5065. Bulk discount policy (not for resale): 10-49 copies 10%, 50-99 copies 20%, 100 or more copies 40%. Canadian and foreign orders must be prepaid in U.S. funds. MasterCard/Visa accepted.